Play Better
CHESS

Rosalyn B. Katz
and David L. Katz

Sterling Publishing Company, Inc.
New York

This book is dedicated to Lynel.

Artwork and Diagrams by Jami L. Anson

Library of Congress Cataloging-in-Publication Data Available

10   9   8   7   6   5   4   3   2   1

Published by Sterling Publishing Company, Inc.
387 Park Avenue South, New York, N.Y. 10016
© 2001 by Rosalyn B. Katz and David L. Katz
Distributed in Canada by Sterling Publishing
C/o Canadian Manda Group, One Atlantic Avenue, Suite 105
Toronto, Ontario, Canada M6K 3E7
Distributed in Great Britain and Europe by Chris Lloyd at Orca Book
Services, Stanley House, Fleets Lane, Poole BH15 3AJ England.
Distributed in Australia by Capricorn Link (Australia) Pty. Ltd.
P.O. Box 704, Windsor, NSW 2756 Australia
Manufactured in the United States of America

Sterling ISBN 0-8069-1561-7

Acknowledgments

We'd like to thank the following chess players for their contributions and help on this book:

Alan Stern   Scott Finlayson
Charles J. Pole   Vincent Klemm
Ernie Johnson   Larry Rasmussen
Dr. Robert Hyde   Maurice Smith

Thanks also to the young people in our pilot group, who gave us such good ideas and great feedback. This includes the students in the Elective Chess Class at IS89 in New York City, Community School District #2 in Manhattan under the Direction of Gary Webster, and those listed below:

Kyle Chmura   Danny Vitale
Nicole Johnson   Terina Johnson

A special thank you is due our editors, Frances Gilbert and Claire Bazinet, for their patience, hard work, and suggestions. Another non-chess player due special thanks is Dr. Al Bazemore.

Jami Anson performed the artwork for this book. Thank you, Jami.

Contents

Foreword

Play Better Chess was written kids like you, who play chess and love the game. This book will give you ideas for winning, not just moving the pieces. You'll learn to analyze—that is, figure out what moves you can make to make your position better. All during the game, there will be choices to make, and you will have control over what happens. Playing chess is fun. Winning at chess is...just great!

Roz Katz and her son David Katz are just the ones to teach you how to win at chess. I've known them both for a very long time as chess players and as people. I most admire Roz for her work in the chess world and the fun she is to be around, and David is a U.S.C.F. Life Master who used to live up here in Toronto. We really miss him at the Scarborough Chess Club. I don't know anyone better to author a book for children on the basic elements of improving chess skills.

Maurice Smith
President, Canadian Chess Federation

A very active tournament director and chess player, Maurice Smith has for many years been a major force in the chess world. He's known, loved, and respected internationally.

Introduction

Our cat plays the piano! Actually, she walks across the keys and makes noise! You want to play chess better than our cat plays the piano.

For this book to work best for you, you need to know how to:

> Move the pieces
> Check, mate, and draw
> Read and write your games

These basics of chess are in our first book, *Start Playing Chess*. If you already know the rules and basics of chess, this book will help you to play chess *better*—and have more fun.

Instead of hitting "wrong notes," making moves that lose you pieces, you will make beautiful moves...and have a terrific time doing it!
Now, let's get started.

Roz and David Katz

Tip: Have your chess set right near you as you read through this book. Then you can move the pieces on the board as you go over the games.

The Pieces and Pawn

Chess play is teamwork, and each piece has its own job to do on the team. Let's look at the chess pieces and the pawn and see how their moves are different and special.

The Knight (N)

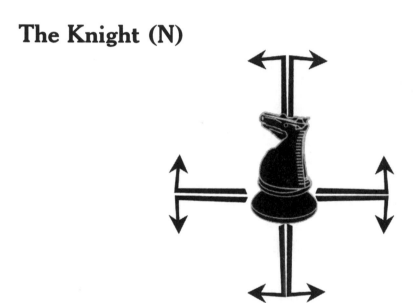

The Knight's move is a jump—two squares one way and one square at right angles (⌐ or L shape).

Strengths

The Knight moves differently than any other piece. It is good in closed positions on the board—when pawns and other pieces are in the way—because it can jump over them. It is the only chess piece that jumps. It is also the only piece that moves in a pattern instead of in a straight line.

Weaknesses

Because of the way it moves, the Knight is slow at moving across the board. It covers only certain squares in a large circle around it, so it needs to be in the middle of things. Look here.

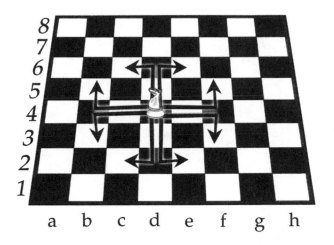

Can you see why it is not good for a Knight to be on the **a** or **h** file, at the sides of the board?

The Knight controls 8 squares when it is on **d4**, but only 4 squares on **h4**.

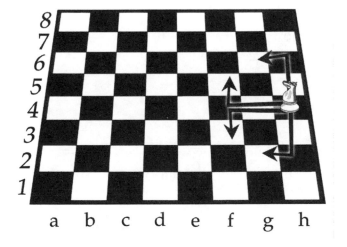

Where would you rather have your Knight?

The Rook (R)

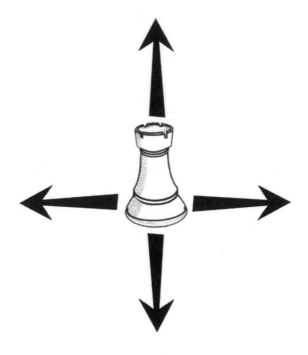

The Rook moves straight ahead in one direction
as many squares as it needs.

Strengths

The Rook moves fast when there is nothing in the way. It is a good piece
to have when the board's ranks and files are mostly empty—open position.

Weaknesses

The Rook is not a good piece in closed positions—when its way is blocked by a lot of other pieces.

Look at the Rooks on this board. Which Rook is placed better?

When you are deciding where to move your Rook, remember that Rooks are better on open files.

The Bishop (B)

The Bishop moves in one direction, diagonally,
as far as it needs to.

Strengths

The Bishop can move
fast and far diagonally.
When you have both
your Bishops, they are
very strong because they
can work as a team: one
covers black squares and
one covers white squares.
Their power is really
cut when you have only
one Bishop.

Weaknesses

A bishop needs long open diagonals in its color.

In a closed position, the Bishop can be blocked by its own pawns.

Each Bishop can move on only half of the board squares, black or white.

The Queen (Q)

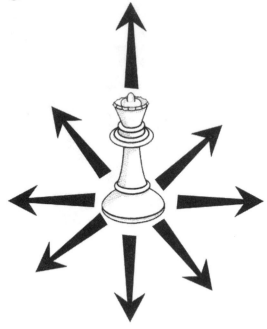

The Queen can move in any direction,
as far as she wants.

Strengths

The Queen is the most powerful piece on the board. She combines the strengths of both the Rook and the Bishop.

She can move fast and in any direction. On the board, the Queen controls more squares than any other piece.

Weaknesses

The Queen can be "chased" by weaker pieces. Try not to move the Queen out too early in the game. The other pieces should come out first.

It is good to have your Queen active in any position, open or closed.

The Pawn

The pawn moves forward only one square at a time. It can move
two squares forward, but only on its opening move.
It moves diagonally to capture.

Strengths
The pawn, by crossing the board, can become a Queen or any other piece.
It can be used to defend other pieces.

Weaknesses
Once the pawn moves forward, it can't go back. So it can be attacked or
blocked easily.

The pawn moves only in one direction, forward, unless it is capturing. But remember the *en passant* "in passing" move? It goes like this.

If a pawn on its starting square moves two squares forward to land next to an enemy pawn, it can be captured as if it had moved only one square.

But, the capture by the enemy pawn must happen *right away*.

Here, the Black d-pawn captures the White c-pawn on **c3**.

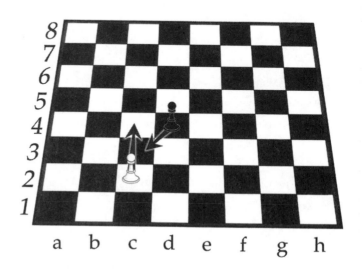

The King (K)

The King can move in any direction,
but only one square at a time.

Strengths
Most important, if you still have your King, you know you haven't lost!

The King can move in any direction. The King can castle. The King is the most help in the ending of the game and in closed positions.

You always want to keep him safe, but remember that the King is a fighting piece—it can capture other pieces.

Weaknesses
The King needs to be protected all the time. It can't move fast enough to run from danger. The King is in most danger in open positions, from pieces that can move far and fast. Keep other pieces nearby to protect him.

On the Board

Chess games are made up of board positions. White and Black pieces move back and forth over the field of play, while pawns just try to get to the other side.

At the beginning of the game, both players move their pawns forward, toward each other, to let their other pieces out. The center of the board can become a pretty busy place. As pawns and pieces are captured, there is more room for the pieces left on the board to move.

Closed Position

Here is a closed position. You can see that many of the pawns are "stuck." Since they can only move forward, they get in the way of the other pieces.

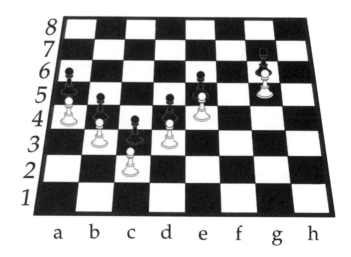

Some players like games where all the pieces are "squished" together and it's hard to move. Closed positions make you think a lot. It's easy to make mistakes when the board is closed, unless you are *really* careful.

Closed Position Stars

Knights and Kings are at their best in closed positions.

Knights can jump over other pieces, so it doesn't matter if something is in the way. Also, since a knight can jump only to certain squares, it doesn't need tons of space around it in order to move, the way other pieces do. Watch out for the Knight on a closed position board!

The King only moves one square at a time in any direction, so it doesn't need lots of open space. In fact, it is the prime target of the opposing pieces so open space is a danger. Make sure your King is protected at all times. Surround it with defenders.

In a closed position game, if an enemy piece should get *too* close, don't forget that the King can also capture!

Open Position

This board shows an open position. With spaces between and in front of pawns, they are free to move forward and to trade. Trade means you take an opponent's pawn diagonally, and your opponent diagonally takes one of yours. On an open board,

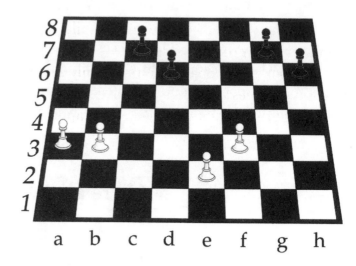

your other pieces can make big moves, racing here and there across the board. Things can get pretty wild.

Sometimes you may play fast, open games. Other times your pawns will be locked with the other player's pawns in a closed position, unable to move. In some games, there aren't any pawns left on the board at all!

When you play, which kind of position is the most fun for you?

Open Position Stars

Bishops, Queens and Rooks are at their best in open positions—they can really use the space and freedom to travel around the board.

Bishops can move as far as you want them to diagonally. Rooks can move as far as you want them to across or up and down the board. The Queen can move as far as you want her to, either up, down, and across the board or diagonally. Beware the Queen in an open position game!

Cool Moves

Some moves just make you want to smile…as long as your pieces aren't the ones that are in danger.

   You look at the board. You suddenly see a move you can make that will attack two pieces at once—even better, two *important* pieces at once! There comes that smile. You can't help but capture one of the two pieces on the play. These kinds of moves definitely add to the fun of chess.

The Fork

A "fork" in chess is when you are able to attack two pieces at the same time with only one of your pieces.

On this board, where should the White Knight go to fork the Black pieces?

If you said d6, you got it!

A "family fork" is when you attack *more* than two pieces at once. Look at the position of the pieces on the board here. A family fork is possible. Do you see it? Okay, then...

Where is the best square to put the Black Knight?

Did you find **f3**? If you did, that's great!

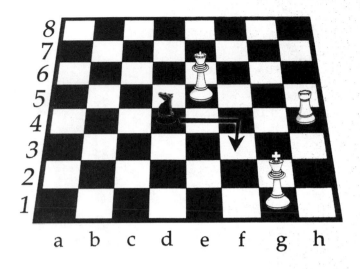

The Skewer

Here, the White Bishop can make a move called a "skewer." A skewer is when one piece is attacked but, if it is moved to safety, the skewering piece attacks a second piece that was behind it!

What is the best square for the Bishop?

You got it again—**g2**! The move "skewers" both pawns. Imagine a stick through them. Doesn't it look like a "shish-kabob?"

Let's look at another.

Skewer these two Rooks with the White Bishop. Move it to **f2**. Even if you don't threaten a check, you will win a Rook.

But look, after your move, the Bishop can be taken! Losing your capturing piece on the very next move is called an "exchange."

So, should you take the Rook if you risk losing the Bishop in the following move? Think about it. Even if you do lose the Bishop, you'll have won a Rook for it.

Capturing a piece worth more than the one you lose when you make the capture is called "winning the exchange." You will win a Rook, and the most Black can get here is a Bishop. Rooks are worth more in pawn value than Bishops, so that is a good move for White.

Value of the Pieces in Pawns

Bishop = 3 pawns
Knight = 3 pawns
Rook = 5 pawns
Queen = 9 pawns
King = priceless!

Discovery

Here is a strong attacking position called a "discovery." Look closely at the board and see if you can find— or discover—it.

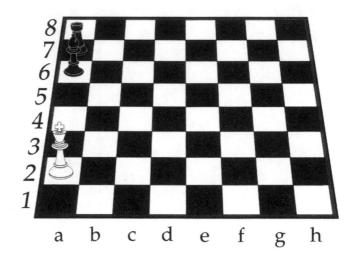

When the Bishop makes a move to anywhere on the board, the Rook will be checking the White King. This is a "discovered check." The Bishop is "pinned." It cannot move away from its spot without putting the King piece behind it in danger.

Double Check

If getting a check is fun, getting a double check is double the fun, right? Here, the Knight to **c5** move is a double check. Both the Knight and the Rook are checking the King.

But, look again! Even better is the Knight to **d4** move. The Rook is still checking the King, but the Knight will capture the Queen on the next move!

How's that for cool?

Double Stuff

In life, sometimes it's better to do one thing at a time. Other times, you can do two things at once—like sing a song while you're drying dishes.

In chess, it's good to have more than one thing happening on the board at a time. Let's look at some ways you can do this "double stuff."

Here, the White Queen is threatening to take Black's pawn on **b7**.

Black moves the Bishop to **c6**, protecting the pawn *AND*

threatening mate with Queen captures **g2** (this is written as Qxg2)!

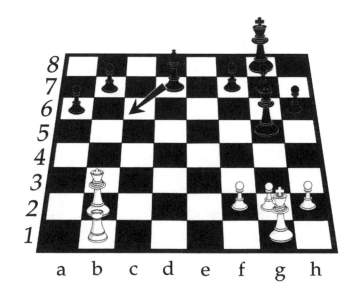

If the White pawn on **f2** moves to **f3**, the Bishop can just take it. The g-pawn is pinned by the Black Queen, so it can't recapture.

The Bishop move (Bc6) by Black causes White big trouble.

When you look at the board, see if you can do two things at once with a move. If you are threatening to take a piece at the same time as you are threatening mate, you will almost definitely win the game.

Here, if you are White, move Qc2, threatening Qxc8 *and* Qxh7 mate! Your opponent now has a choice to make— either save the King, or save the piece.

A Fun Game

Now, we'll go over a game one move at a time. The shaded moves show the move you are looking at in the diagram next to it. You can use your chessboard to go over the moves, or just use your book. Make sure to look at every move and decide how you would move if the game were yours.

This game was played in 1989 at the U. S. Amateur Team Championship in New Jersey. This is a giant tournament that is played in February every year on President's Weekend. More than 1,000 players come every year to play in this tournament. Lots of kids play in this event.

In the game, White was played by David Koenig. Black was played by Charles Pole.

Chess Notation Code

K	King	!	good move
Q	Queen	!!	great move
R	Rook	?	bad move
B	Bishop	??	rotten move
N	Knight	?!	may be bad move
x	captures or takes	!?	interesting move
+	check	0-0	castle kingside
++	checkmate	0-0-0	castle queenside

1 e4

1 ... e5

This game uses a popular opening called the Ruy Lopez.

	White	Black
1	e4	e5
2	Nf3	Nc6
3	Bb5	a6
4	Ba4	d6
5	c3	f5
6	ef5	Bf5
7	d4	e4
8	Ng5	Be7
9	Qb3	Bg5
10	Bg5	Qg5
11	Qb7	Qc1+
12	Ke2	Qh1
13	Qa8+	Kf7
14	Bc6	Ne7
15	Qh8	Nc6
16	Qa8	Bg4+
17	f3	ef3+
18	gf3	Qf3+
	resigns	

2 Nf3

	White	Black
1	e4	e5
2	Nf3	Nc6
3	Bb5	a6
4	Ba4	d6
5	c3	f5
6	ef5	Bf5
7	d4	e4
8	Ng5	Be7
9	Qb3	Bg5
10	Bg5	Qg5
11	Qb7	Qc1+
12	Ke2	Qh1
13	Qa8+	Kf7
14	Bc6	Ne7
15	Qh8	Nc6
16	Qa8	Bg4+
17	f3	ef3+
18	gf3	Qf3+
	resigns	

2 ... Nc6

3 Bb5

3 ... a6

	White	Black
1	e4	e5
2	Nf3	Nc6
3	Bb5	a6
4	Ba4	d6
5	c3	f5
6	ef5	Bf5
7	d4	e4
8	Ng5	Be7
9	Qb3	Bg5
10	Bg5	Qg5
11	Qb7	Qc1+
12	Ke2	Qh1
13	Qa8+	Kf7
14	Bc6	Ne7
15	Qh8	Nc6
16	Qa8	Bg4+
17	f3	ef3+
18	gf3	Qf3+
	resigns	

4 Ba4

4 ... d6

	White	Black
1	e4	e5
2	Nf3	Nc6
3	Bb5	a6
4	Ba4	d6
5	c3	f5
6	ef5	Bf5
7	d4	e4
8	Ng5	Be7
9	Qb3	Bg5
10	Bg5	Qg5
11	Qb7	Qc1+
12	Ke2	Qh1
13	Qa8+	Kf7
14	Bc6	Ne7
15	Qh8	Nc6
16	Qa8	Bg4+
17	f3	ef3+
18	gf3	Qf3+
	resigns	

5 c3

5 ... f5

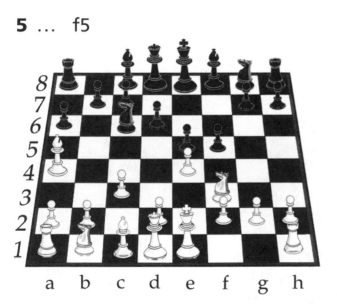

	White	Black
1	e4	e5
2	Nf3	Nc6
3	Bb5	a6
4	Ba4	d6
5	c3	f5
6	ef5	Bf5
7	d4	e4
8	Ng5	Be7
9	Qb3	Bg5
10	Bg5	Qg5
11	Qb7	Qc1+
12	Ke2	Qh1
13	Qa8+	Kf7
14	Bc6	Ne7
15	Qh8	Nc6
16	Qa8	Bg4+
17	f3	ef3+
18	gf3	Qf3+
	resigns	

These first five moves are very ordinary. Lots of books show games with this position. Black is trying for an open position on this move.

6 ef5

6 ... Bf5

	White	Black
1	e4	e5
2	Nf3	Nc6
3	Bb5	a6
4	Ba4	d6
5	c3	f5
6	ef5	Bf5
7	d4	e4
8	Ng5	Be7
9	Qb3	Bg5
10	Bg5	Qg5
11	Qb7	Qc1+
12	Ke2	Qh1
13	Qa8+	Kf7
14	Bc6	Ne7
15	Qh8	Nc6
16	Qa8	Bg4+
17	f3	ef3+
18	gf3	Qf3+
	resigns	

7 d4
White is trying to open the position.

7 ... e4
Instead of taking White's pawn, Black attacks the Knight.

	White	Black
1	e4	e5
2	Nf3	Nc6
3	Bb5	a6
4	Ba4	d6
5	c3	f5
6	ef5	Bf5
7	d4	e4
8	Ng5	Be7
9	Qb3	Bg5
10	Bg5	Qg5
11	Qb7	Qc1+
12	Ke2	Qh1
13	Qa8+	Kf7
14	Bc6	Ne7
15	Qh8	Nc6
16	Qa8	Bg4+
17	f3	ef3+
18	gf3	Qf3+
	resigns	

8 Ng5

8 ... Be7

Black attacks the Knight with the Queen
and the Bishop.

	White	Black
1	e4	e5
2	Nf3	Nc6
3	Bb5	a6
4	Ba4	d6
5	c3	f5
6	ef5	Bf5
7	d4	e4
8	Ng5	Be7
9	Qb3	Bg5
10	Bg5	Qg5
11	Qb7	Qc1+
12	Ke2	Qh1
13	Qa8+	Kf7
14	Bc6	Ne7
15	Qh8	Nc6
16	Qa8	Bg4+
17	f3	ef3+
18	gf3	Qf3+
	resigns	

9 Qb3

Instead of protecting the Knight, White attacks. It's a double threat! The Queen threatens to check at **f7** and to capture the pawn on **b7**.

9 ... Bg5

Black ignores both threats, captures the White Knight, and attacks the Bishop on **c1**.

	White	Black
1	e4	e5
2	Nf3	Nc6
3	Bb5	a6
4	Ba4	d6
5	c3	f5
6	ef5	Bf5
7	d4	e4
8	Ng5	Be7
9	Qb3	Bg5
10	Bg5	Qg5
11	Qb7	Qc1+
12	Ke2	Qh1
13	Qa8+	Kf7
14	Bc6	Ne7
15	Qh8	Nc6
16	Qa8	Bg4+
17	f3	ef3+
18	gf3	Qf3+
	resigns	

10 Bg5

White exchanges Bishops.

10 ... Qg5

	White	Black
1	e4	e5
2	Nf3	Nc6
3	Bb5	a6
4	Ba4	d6
5	c3	f5
6	ef5	Bf5
7	d4	e4
8	Ng5	Be7
9	Qb3	Bg5
10	Bg5	Qg5
11	Qb7	Qc1+
12	Ke2	Qh1
13	Qa8+	Kf7
14	Bc6	Ne7
15	Qh8	Nc6
16	Qa8	Bg4+
17	f3	ef3+
18	gf3	Qf3+
	resigns	

11 Qb7

The Queen takes the pawn and threatens the
Rook on **a8** or the Knight on **c6**.

11 ... Qc1+

Instead of trying to protect the pieces,
Black attacks the White King! Check!

	White	Black
1	e4	e5
2	Nf3	Nc6
3	Bb5	a6
4	Ba4	d6
5	c3	f5
6	ef5	Bf5
7	d4	e4
8	Ng5	Be7
9	Qb3	Bg5
10	Bg5	Qg5
11	Qb7	Qc1+
12	Ke2	Qh1
13	Qa8+	Kf7
14	Bc6	Ne7
15	Qh8	Nc6
16	Qa8	Bg4+
17	f3	ef3+
18	gf3	Qf3+
	resigns	

12 Ke2

The move, the only one for the White King, leaves the White Rook hanging.

12 ... Qh1

The Black Queen captures the White Rook on **h1**. Now the Black Rook on **a8** and the Black Knight on **c6** are both hanging. They are completely unprotected.

	White	Black
1	e4	e5
2	Nf3	Nc6
3	Bb5	a6
4	Ba4	d6
5	c3	f5
6	ef5	Bf5
7	d4	e4
8	Ng5	Be7
9	Qb3	Bg5
10	Bg5	Qg5
11	Qb7	Qc1+
12	Ke2	Qh1
13	Qa8+	Kf7
14	Bc6	Ne7
15	Qh8	Nc6
16	Qa8	Bg4+
17	f3	ef3+
18	gf3	Qf3+
	resigns	

Plenty of stuff to look at in this game, isn't there?

13 Qa8+

White must feel good about getting Black's Rook and checking at the same time.

13 ... Kf7

	White	Black
1	e4	e5
2	Nf3	Nc6
3	Bb5	a6
4	Ba4	d6
5	c3	f5
6	ef5	Bf5
7	d4	e4
8	Ng5	Be7
9	Qb3	Bg5
10	Bg5	Qg5
11	Qb7	Qc1+
12	Ke2	Qh1
13	Qa8+	Kf7
14	Bc6	Ne7
15	Qh8	Nc6
16	Qa8	Bg4+
17	f3	ef3+
18	gf3	Qf3+
	resigns	

14 Bc6

Oops! White captured Black's Bishop.

14 ... Ne7

Black lets White capture the Rook, but gets another piece into the fight.

	White	Black
1	e4	e5
2	Nf3	Nc6
3	Bb5	a6
4	Ba4	d6
5	c3	f5
6	ef5	Bf5
7	d4	e4
8	Ng5	Be7
9	Qb3	Bg5
10	Bg5	Qg5
11	Qb7	Qc1+
12	Ke2	Qh1
13	Qa8+	Kf7
14	Bc6	Ne7
15	Qh8	Nc6
16	Qa8	Bg4+
17	f3	ef3+
18	gf3	Qf3+
	resigns	

15 Qh8

And another Rook bites the dust.

15 ... Nc6

	White	Black
1	e4	e5
2	Nf3	Nc6
3	Bb5	a6
4	Ba4	d6
5	c3	f5
6	ef5	Bf5
7	d4	e4
8	Ng5	Be7
9	Qb3	Bg5
10	Bg5	Qg5
11	Qb7	Qc1+
12	Ke2	Qh1
13	Qa8+	Kf7
14	Bc6	Ne7
15	Qh8	Nc6
16	Qa8	Bg4+
17	f3	ef3+
18	gf3	Qf3+
	resigns	

16 Qa8
White attacks the Knight.

16 ... Bg4+
Black checks with the Bishop.

	White	Black
1	e4	e5
2	Nf3	Nc6
3	Bb5	a6
4	Ba4	d6
5	c3	f5
6	ef5	Bf5
7	d4	e4
8	Ng5	Be7
9	Qb3	Bg5
10	Bg5	Qg5
11	Qb7	Qc1+
12	Ke2	Qh1
13	Qa8+	Kf7
14	Bc6	Ne7
15	Qh8	Nc6
16	Qa8	Bg4+
17	f3	ef3+
18	gf3	Qf3+
	resigns	

17 f3

White is in big trouble. The check is
blocked with the White pawn.

17 ... ef3+

Black captures the pawn with a check.

	White	Black
1	e4	e5
2	Nf3	Nc6
3	Bb5	a6
4	Ba4	d6
5	c3	f5
6	ef5	Bf5
7	d4	e4
8	Ng5	Be7
9	Qb3	Bg5
10	Bg5	Qg5
11	Qb7	Qc1+
12	Ke2	Qh1
13	Qa8+	Kf7
14	Bc6	Ne7
15	Qh8	Nc6
16	Qa8	Bg4+
17	f3	ef3+
18	gf3	Qf3+
	resigns	

18 gf3

White recaptures and again blocks the check.

18 ... Qf3+

Black now has two pieces attacking the pawn.

	White	Black
1	e4	e5
2	Nf3	Nc6
3	Bb5	a6
4	Ba4	d6
5	c3	f5
6	ef5	Bf5
7	d4	e4
8	Ng5	Be7
9	Qb3	Bg5
10	Bg5	Qg5
11	Qb7	Qc1+
12	Ke2	Qh1
13	Qa8+	Kf7
14	Bc6	Ne7
15	Qh8	Nc6
16	Qa8	Bg4+
17	f3	ef3+
18	gf3	Qf3+
	resigns	

White sees no way to stop checkmate.
At what would have been move 19,
White resigns.

Look again, here, at the last board.

If play had gone on, after the White King
moves to **d2**, the Black Queen would check
at **e2**. The White King must then go to **c1**,
and the Queen would checkmate on **d1**.
End of story.

		White	Black
1		e4	e5
2		Nf3	Nc6
3		Bb5	a6
4		Ba4	d6
5		c3	f5
6		ef5	Bf5
7		d4	e4
8		Ng5	Be7
9		Qb3	Bg5
10		Bg5	Qg5
11		Qb7	Qc1+
12		Ke2	Qh1
13		Qa8+	Kf7
14		Bc6	Ne7
15		Qh8	Nc6
16		Qa8	Bg4+
17		f3	ef3+
18		gf3	Qf3+
		resigns	

A Weird Game

Here, we'll go over another game. You'll see that it's really different from the game we just went through. Go over it in the same way you did the last one—one move at a time.

This game was played in 1975. Pete Tamburro played White and Vincent Klemm played Black. Both players grew to be very important in the chess world. Pete now teaches chess and writes articles about chess. Vincent is a Master Chess Player and works at the United States Chess Federation.

1 e4

1 … c5

	White	Black
1	e4	c5
2	c3	g6
3	d4	cd4
4	cd4	d5
5	e5	Nc6
6	Nc3	Nh6
7	h4	Nf5
8	Be3	h5
9	Rc1	Bg7
10	Nf3	0-0
11	Bb5	Bd7!
12	Nd5	Qa5+
13	Nc3	Ne5!!
14	de5	Bb5
15	Qd5	a6
16	a4	Rfd8
17	Qc5	Rac8
18	Qb6	Ne3!
19	Qe3	Rd3
20	Qe4	Rdc3
21	bc3	Rc3
22	Rc3	Qc3
23	Nd2	Qc1 mate

This opening is called the Sicilian Defense. Openings using the word "defense" mean the Black moves set the tone for the whole game.

2 c3

2 ... g6

	White	Black
1	e4	c5
2	c3	g6
3	d4	cd4
4	cd4	d5
5	e5	Nc6
6	Nc3	Nh6
7	h4	Nf5
8	Be3	h5
9	Rc1	Bg7
10	Nf3	0-0
11	Bb5	Bd7!
12	Nd5	Qa5+
13	Nc3	Ne5!!
14	de5	Bb5
15	Qd5	a6
16	a4	Rfd8
17	Qc5	Rac8
18	Qb6	Ne3!
19	Qe3	Rd3
20	Qe4	Rdc3
21	bc3	Rc3
22	Rc3	Qc3
23	Nd2	Qc1 mate

Look at all the squares where White's Bishops can go. It's great for White if this is an open game.

3 d4

3 ... cd4

Black's Bishops also have plenty of room to move.

	White	Black
1	e4	c5
2	c3	g6
3	d4	cd4
4	cd4	d5
5	e5	Nc6
6	Nc3	Nh6
7	h4	Nf5
8	Be3	h5
9	Rc1	Bg7
10	Nf3	0-0
11	Bb5	Bd7!
12	Nd5	Qa5+
13	Nc3	Ne5!!
14	de5	Bb5
15	Qd5	a6
16	a4	Rfd8
17	Qc5	Rac8
18	Qb6	Ne3!
19	Qe3	Rd3
20	Qe4	Rdc3
21	bc3	Rc3
22	Rc3	Qc3
23	Nd2	Qc1 mate

4 cd4

4 ... d5

	White	Black
1	e4	c5
2	c3	g6
3	d4	cd4
4	cd4	d5
5	e5	Nc6
6	Nc3	Nh6
7	h4	Nf5
8	Be3	h5
9	Rc1	Bg7
10	Nf3	0-0
11	Bb5	Bd7!
12	Nd5	Qa5+
13	Nc3	Ne5!!
14	de5	Bb5
15	Qd5	a6
16	a4	Rfd8
17	Qc5	Rac8
18	Qb6	Ne3!
19	Qe3	Rd3
20	Qe4	Rdc3
21	bc3	Rc3
22	Rc3	Qc3
23	Nd2	Qc1 mate

5 e5
White closes the position up a little.

5 ... Nc6
Black might have some trouble moving around.

	White	Black
1	e4	c5
2	c3	g6
3	d4	cd4
4	cd4	d5
5	e5	Nc6
6	Nc3	Nh6
7	h4	Nf5
8	Be3	h5
9	Rc1	Bg7
10	Nf3	0-0
11	Bb5	Bd7!
12	Nd5	Qa5+
13	Nc3	Ne5!!
14	de5	Bb5
15	Qd5	a6
16	a4	Rfd8
17	Qc5	Rac8
18	Qb6	Ne3!
19	Qe3	Rd3
20	Qe4	Rdc3
21	bc3	Rc3
22	Rc3	Qc3
23	Nd2	Qc1 mate

6 Nc3

6 ... Nh6

The Black Knight is on a bad square at **h6**, but the plan is to move it to **f5** as soon as possible.

	White	Black
1	e4	c5
2	c3	g6
3	d4	cd4
4	cd4	d5
5	e5	Nc6
6	Nc3	Nh6
7	h4	Nf5
8	Be3	h5
9	Rc1	Bg7
10	Nf3	0-0
11	Bb5	Bd7!
12	Nd5	Qa5+
13	Nc3	Ne5!!
14	de5	Bb5
15	Qd5	a6
16	a4	Rfd8
17	Qc5	Rac8
18	Qb6	Ne3!
19	Qe3	Rd3
20	Qe4	Rdc3
21	bc3	Rc3
22	Rc3	Qc3
23	Nd2	Qc1 mate

7 h4

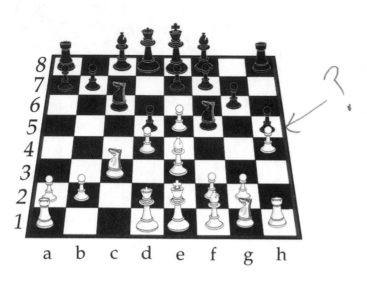

7 … Nf5

Now Black is attacking the pawn on **d4**
with two pieces.

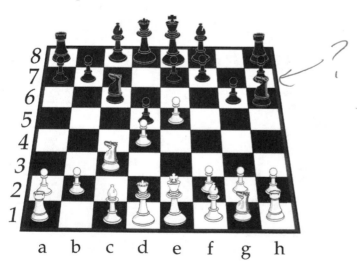

	White	Black
1	e4	c5
2	c3	g6
3	d4	cd4
4	cd4	d5
5	e5	Nc6
6	Nc3	Nh6
7	h4	Nf5
8	Be3	h5
9	Rc1	Bg7
10	Nf3	0-0
11	Bb5	Bd7!
12	Nd5	Qa5+
13	Nc3	Ne5!!
14	de5	Bb5
15	Qd5	a6
16	a4	Rfd8
17	Qc5	Rac8
18	Qb6	Ne3!
19	Qe3	Rd3
20	Qe4	Rdc3
21	bc3	Rc3
22	Rc3	Qc3
23	Nd2	Qc1 mate

8 Be3

White protects the pawn.

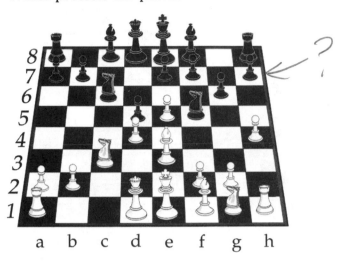

8 ... h5

Black keeps the White g-pawn from attacking the Knight, and keeps the h-pawn from moving forward.

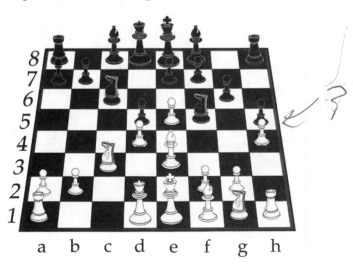

	White	Black
1	e4	c5
2	c3	g6
3	d4	cd4
4	cd4	d5
5	e5	Nc6
6	Nc3	Nh6
7	h4	Nf5
8	Be3	h5
9	Rc1	Bg7
10	Nf3	0-0
11	Bb5	Bd7!
12	Nd5	Qa5+
13	Nc3	Ne5!!
14	de5	Bb5
15	Qd5	a6
16	a4	Rfd8
17	Qc5	Rac8
18	Qb6	Ne3!
19	Qe3	Rd3
20	Qe4	Rdc3
21	bc3	Rc3
22	Rc3	Qc3
23	Nd2	Qc1 mate

9 Rc1

9 ... Bg7

	White	Black
1	e4	c5
2	c3	g6
3	d4	cd4
4	cd4	d5
5	e5	Nc6
6	Nc3	Nh6
7	h4	Nf5
8	Be3	h5
9	Rc1	Bg7
10	Nf3	0-0
11	Bb5	Bd7!
12	Nd5	Qa5+
13	Nc3	Ne5!!
14	de5	Bb5
15	Qd5	a6
16	a4	Rfd8
17	Qc5	Rac8
18	Qb6	Ne3!
19	Qe3	Rd3
20	Qe4	Rdc3
21	bc3	Rc3
22	Rc3	Qc3
23	Nd2	Qc1 mate

-62-

10 Nf3

10 ... 0-0

A kingside castle. Black is setting a trap here. Watch carefully.

	White	Black
1	e4	c5
2	c3	g6
3	d4	cd4
4	cd4	d5
5	e5	Nc6
6	Nc3	Nh6
7	h4	Nf5
8	Be3	h5
9	Rc1	Bg7
10	Nf3	0-0
11	Bb5	Bd7!
12	Nd5	Qa5+
13	Nc3	Ne5!!
14	de5	Bb5
15	Qd5	a6
16	a4	Rfd8
17	Qc5	Rac8
18	Qb6	Ne3!
19	Qe3	Rd3
20	Qe4	Rdc3
21	bc3	Rc3
22	Rc3	Qc3
23	Nd2	Qc1 mate

11 Bb5

11 ... Bd7!

	White	Black
1	e4	c5
2	c3	g6
3	d4	cd4
4	cd4	d5
5	e5	Nc6
6	Nc3	Nh6
7	h4	Nf5
8	Be3	h5
9	Rc1	Bg7
10	Nf3	0-0
11	Bb5	Bd7!
12	Nd5	Qa5+
13	Nc3	Ne5!!
14	de5	Bb5
15	Qd5	a6
16	a4	Rfd8
17	Qc5	Rac8
18	Qb6	Ne3!
19	Qe3	Rd3
20	Qe4	Rdc3
21	bc3	Rc3
22	Rc3	Qc3
23	Nd2	Qc1 mate

12 Nd5

12 ... Qa5+

White is being really greedy, but Black shows it won't work here. This is known as "refuting" a move. You're telling the opponent "ha – that didn't work."

	White	Black
1	e4	c5
2	c3	g6
3	d4	cd4
4	cd4	d5
5	e5	Nc6
6	Nc3	Nh6
7	h4	Nf5
8	Be3	h5
9	Rc1	Bg7
10	Nf3	0-0
11	Bb5	Bd7!
12	Nd5	Qa5+
13	Nc3	Ne5!!
14	de5	Bb5
15	Qd5	a6
16	a4	Rfd8
17	Qc5	Rac8
18	Qb6	Ne3!
19	Qe3	Rd3
20	Qe4	Rdc3
21	bc3	Rc3
22	Rc3	Qc3
23	Nd2	Qc1 mate

13 Nc3

13 ... Ne5!!
It looks as if Black is sacrificing the Knight, giving it away. But the White Bishop on **b5** is being attacked by two pieces.

	White	Black
1	e4	c5
2	c3	g6
3	d4	cd4
4	cd4	d5
5	e5	Nc6
6	Nc3	Nh6
7	h4	Nf5
8	Be3	h5
9	Rc1	Bg7
10	Nf3	0-0
11	Bb5	Bd7!
12	Nd5	Qa5+
13	Nc3	Ne5!!
14	de5	Bb5
15	Qd5	a6
16	a4	Rfd8
17	Qc5	Rac8
18	Qb6	Ne3!
19	Qe3	Rd3
20	Qe4	Rdc3
21	bc3	Rc3
22	Rc3	Qc3
23	Nd2	Qc1 mate

14 de5
White wins the Knight.

14 ... Bb5
But White also loses the Bishop.

	White	Black
1	e4	c5
2	c3	g6
3	d4	cd4
4	cd4	d5
5	e5	Nc6
6	Nc3	Nh6
7	h4	Nf5
8	Be3	h5
9	Rc1	Bg7
10	Nf3	0-0
11	Bb5	Bd7!
12	Nd5	Qa5+
13	Nc3	Ne5!!
14	de5	Bb5
15	Qd5	a6
16	a4	Rfd8
17	Qc5	Rac8
18	Qb6	Ne3!
19	Qe3	Rd3
20	Qe4	Rdc3
21	bc3	Rc3
22	Rc3	Qc3
23	Nd2	Qc1 mate

15 Qd5

Now White attacks the Black Bishop with two pieces.

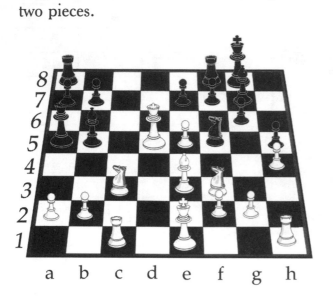

15 ... a6

Black protects the Bishop.

	White	Black
1	e4	c5
2	c3	g6
3	d4	cd4
4	cd4	d5
5	e5	Nc6
6	Nc3	Nh6
7	h4	Nf5
8	Be3	h5
9	Rc1	Bg7
10	Nf3	0-0
11	Bb5	Bd7!
12	Nd5	Qa5+
13	Nc3	Ne5!!
14	de5	Bb5
15	Qd5	a6
16	a4	Rfd8
17	Qc5	Rac8
18	Qb6	Ne3!
19	Qe3	Rd3
20	Qe4	Rdc3
21	bc3	Rc3
22	Rc3	Qc3
23	Nd2	Qc1 mate

16 a4

It looks as if White has won the Black Bishop.
It is pinned because, if it moves, the Black
Queen is attacked.

16 ... Rfd8

Black chases the White Queen from **d5**.

	White	Black
1	e4	c5
2	c3	g6
3	d4	cd4
4	cd4	d5
5	e5	Nc6
6	Nc3	Nh6
7	h4	Nf5
8	Be3	h5
9	Rc1	Bg7
10	Nf3	0-0
11	Bb5	Bd7!
12	Nd5	Qa5+
13	Nc3	Ne5!!
14	de5	Bb5
15	Qd5	a6
16	a4	Rfd8
17	Qc5	Rac8
18	Qb6	Ne3!
19	Qe3	Rd3
20	Qe4	Rdc3
21	bc3	Rc3
22	Rc3	Qc3
23	Nd2	Qc1 mate

17 Qc5
White is still pinning the Bishop.

17 ... Rac8
Black chases the White Queen again.

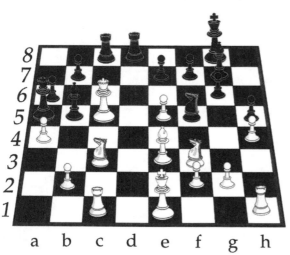

	White	Black
1	e4	c5
2	c3	g6
3	d4	cd4
4	cd4	d5
5	e5	Nc6
6	Nc3	Nh6
7	h4	Nf5
8	Be3	h5
9	Rc1	Bg7
10	Nf3	0-0
11	Bb5	Bd7!
12	Nd5	Qa5+
13	Nc3	Ne5!!
14	de5	Bb5
15	Qd5	a6
16	a4	Rfd8
17	Qc5	Rac8
18	Qb6	Ne3!
19	Qe3	Rd3
20	Qe4	Rdc3
21	bc3	Rc3
22	Rc3	Qc3
23	Nd2	Qc1 mate

18 Qb6
Looks like Black will be forced to trade Queens.

18 ... Ne3!
Surprise! Black did not take the Queen. On the next move, White will not be able to move Qxa5, because of Nxg2++.

	White	Black
1	e4	c5
2	c3	g6
3	d4	cd4
4	cd4	d5
5	e5	Nc6
6	Nc3	Nh6
7	h4	Nf5
8	Be3	h5
9	Rc1	Bg7
10	Nf3	0-0
11	Bb5	Bd7!
12	Nd5	Qa5+
13	Nc3	Ne5!!
14	de5	Bb5
15	Qd5	a6
16	a4	Rfd8
17	Qc5	Rac8
18	Qb6	Ne3!
19	Qe3	Rd3
20	Qe4	Rdc3
21	bc3	Rc3
22	Rc3	Qc3
23	Nd2	Qc1 mate

19 Qe3

The Queen had to take the Knight.

19 … Rd3

Black keeps chasing the White Queen. The Knight on **c3** is attacked by three pieces!

	White	Black
1	e4	c5
2	c3	g6
3	d4	cd4
4	cd4	d5
5	e5	Nc6
6	Nc3	Nh6
7	h4	Nf5
8	Be3	h5
9	Rc1	Bg7
10	Nf3	0-0
11	Bb5	Bd7!
12	Nd5	Qa5+
13	Nc3	Ne5!!
14	de5	Bb5
15	Qd5	a6
16	a4	Rfd8
17	Qc5	Rac8
18	Qb6	Ne3!
19	Qe3	Rd3
20	Qe4	Rdc3
21	bc3	Rc3
22	Rc3	Qc3
23	Nd2	Qc1 mate

20 Qe4

20 ... Rdc3

Black sacrifices a Rook for a Knight in order to checkmate White. Can you figure out what is going to happen here?

	White	Black
1	e4	c5
2	c3	g6
3	d4	cd4
4	cd4	d5
5	e5	Nc6
6	Nc3	Nh6
7	h4	Nf5
8	Be3	h5
9	Rc1	Bg7
10	Nf3	0-0
11	Bb5	Bd7!
12	Nd5	Qa5+
13	Nc3	Ne5!!
14	de5	Bb5
15	Qd5	a6
16	a4	Rfd8
17	Qc5	Rac8
18	Qb6	Ne3!
19	Qe3	Rd3
20	Qe4	Rdc3
21	bc3	Rc3
22	Rc3	Qc3
23	Nd2	Qc1 mate

21 bc3

21 … Rc3

Now Black is threatening a discovered check.
When the Rook moves, the Queen will be
checking the White King. We talked about
discovered checks before.

	White	Black
1	e4	c5
2	c3	g6
3	d4	cd4
4	cd4	d5
5	e5	Nc6
6	Nc3	Nh6
7	h4	Nf5
8	Be3	h5
9	Rc1	Bg7
10	Nf3	0-0
11	Bb5	Bd7!
12	Nd5	Qa5+
13	Nc3	Ne5!!
14	de5	Bb5
15	Qd5	a6
16	a4	Rfd8
17	Qc5	Rac8
18	Qb6	Ne3!
19	Qe3	Rd3
20	Qe4	Rdc3
21	bc3	Rc3
22	Rc3	Qc3
23	Nd2	Qc1 mate

22 Rc3

White stops the discovered check by taking the Rook.

22 ... Qc3+

The Queen checks and is threatening mate.

	White	Black
1	e4	c5
2	c3	g6
3	d4	cd4
4	cd4	d5
5	e5	Nc6
6	Nc3	Nh6
7	h4	Nf5
8	Be3	h5
9	Rc1	Bg7
10	Nf3	0-0
11	Bb5	Bd7!
12	Nd5	Qa5+
13	Nc3	Ne5!!
14	de5	Bb5
15	Qd5	a6
16	a4	Rfd8
17	Qc5	Rac8
18	Qb6	Ne3!
19	Qe3	Rd3
20	Qe4	Rdc3
21	bc3	Rc3
22	Rc3	Qc3+
23	Nd2	Qc1 mate

23 Nd2

23 ... Qc1 mate

The good development of Black's pieces has won this game. White is "busted."

	White	Black
1	e4	c5
2	c3	g6
3	d4	cd4
4	cd4	d5
5	e5	Nc6
6	Nc3	Nh6
7	h4	Nf5
8	Be3	h5
9	Rc1	Bg7
10	Nf3	0-0
11	Bb5	Bd7!
12	Nd5	Qa5+
13	Nc3	Ne5!!
14	de5	Bb5
15	Qd5	a6
16	a4	Rfd8
17	Qc5	Rac8
18	Qb6	Ne3!
19	Qe3	Rd3
20	Qe4	Rdc3
21	bc3	Rc3
22	Rc3	Qc3
23	Nd2	Qc1 mate

Finishing the Job

Games do not play themselves. I once had a great game going and I said to myself, "This is so good, it plays itself." Guess what? I lost. The game didn't play itself.

Even if it looks as if you are way out ahead—you're pretty sure of your win—you still need to finish off your opponent. That final checkmate is really important.

Take a look at the pieces on this board. White seems to be winning. But if it is Black's turn to move now, he can't. There are NO legal moves, so it is a stalemate. No one wins. Even though White worked really hard to get this position, it's just a draw. Don't let this happen to you. There are strategies to getting that checkmate—and winning the game.

Mating with Rook and King

If you have a Rook and a King against just a King, you can always win. You just need to know how.

The steps to winning in this position are:

1. Use the Rook to keep the King on one side of the board. The Rook makes a wall or fence that keeps the King from escaping.
2. Walk your King along this wall until the enemy King is forced right in front.
3. Move your Rook to the other side of the board if it is attacked.
4. Wait for a move with your Rook, to make sure your King is in the right place. Don't be afraid to take your time.
5. Push the wall so that the enemy King runs out of space.

Now, let's go over the moves one by one.

Use the Rook to keep your opponent's King on one side of the board. In your mind, see a wall or fence that is keeping the King from escaping.

Here, the Black Rook on **a5** controls rank 5. The Black King is pushing the White King into the corner. Don't let it near the center of the board to escape.

How would you move for Black in this position?

The Black King should move to **d4**. This is the best move. Then, if White's move is Kd6, Ra6+.

Remember to use the Rook to guard the fence, and keep pushing that enemy King back into the corner.

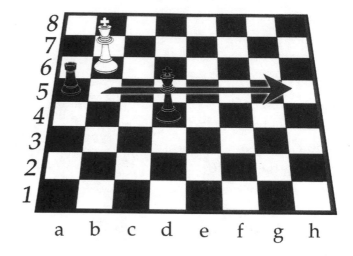

You want to keep pushing the White King back until there is no way for it to escape.

Keep your King following that White King, until the Rook can "squish" the King again…

…by moving to the 6th rank. This forces the White King back to the 7th rank with Rg6+

You can mate the same way if you have a Queen instead of a Rook.

But be
careful
NOT to
stalemate.

In the position here, if it is Black's move, the game is a stalemate.

Black has NO legal moves.

This is much better.

Checkmate!!

King and Pawn Against King

When one player has only a King and a pawn and the other has just a King, it is a hard game to win. Many times the game will draw. If your pawn is in the middle of the board, your chances of winning are better than if the pawn is on the side of the board. Here are some tips to help you.

    1. Protect your pawn with the King.

    2. Get your King in front of your pawn. That way, you can force the enemy King away.

    3. Queen the pawn by getting to the back rank.

Once you move the White King to in front of the White pawn, you know you have a win.

The White King must
move to the side so
that the pawn can
become a Queen.

You can see that
the White pawn is
moving forward.
The move checks
the Black King and
pushes it away.

Again, the pawn checks the Black King and gets closer to making a new Queen. There is no way to stop this pawn.

Yes!! Finally a new Queen! You need to be really patient in this kind of position.

The rest of the game should be easy. Just remember to squish the Black King.

Take your time. Be patient.
Don't stalemate.

How to Learn More

Let's look at ways to get better at chess. People have different ways to do this. All the chess players I've met want to get better, but they like to "do their own thing." Some read chess books. Some take lessons from teachers. I just love to play, and when you play people who are better players than you are, you learn from them.

So, the best way I know to learn chess is to play as much as you can. When you do play, really have fun with the game. That way, practicing is terrific instead of a chore.

Also, when you can, try to play with people who are really good players. You may lose every game, but you will learn so much from playing these people. Then, suddenly, one day—Surprise! You just may win!

Besides playing every chance you get, here are ways to get better at chess.

Join an Organization or Club

Join the United States Chess Federation (USCF), the Canadian Chess Federation, or some such organization where you live. The USCF has a scholastic membership for young players. It includes a monthly magazine with all kinds of games, quizzes, information, and tournament announcements. You can also find teachers and clubs listed.

Many schools have chess clubs. They often meet after classes. If your school doesn't have a club, maybe a teacher or parent will agree to start one.

Take Part in Tournaments

Tournaments give players a chance to compete over the board, face to face. After the game, they get to talk about what happened, and go over their game together. Players call this a *postmortem*. It really helps you improve your game. You learn what your mistakes were—and you can fix them!

Play Chess Over the Internet

Use the Internet to play or to learn more about the game. Games are going on every day and all the time—after all, chess is played around the world.

Use your favorite search engine and enter words such as chess, scholastic, kids, and play. My own favorite search engine is http://www.Google.com

Some helpful sites are:

United States Chess Federation: http://www.uschess.org The USCF also has a scholastic web page, and their *School Mates* magazine can be found at http://www.uschess.org/about/smates.html

Canadian Scholastic Chess: http://www.chess-math.org

Chess Federation of Canada: http://www.chess.ca

Chess for Kids: http://www.chessforkids.on.ca Try this site. It's great. They teach chess to kids and talk about special chess stuff all through Ontario, Canada.

Yahoo: Through www.Yahoo.com, you can find hundreds of chess clubs, and all levels of play.

Use Computer Programs

There are computer programs you can buy to teach you and to help you practice. Chess Base lets you go over games from really good players. Chess Master 6000 is a good program to play against.

Chess computers that you can hold in your hand are great fun to play with and are especially good on long car trips.

Take Lessons with a Teacher

A teacher can go over your games with you and help you to get better.

If you live near a big city, it's usually easy to find a chess teacher.

Study with a Friend

It's great to have a friend that you can learn with. You can practice together and talk about your moves.

Go Over Books and Newspapers

Bookstores carry many chess books at all levels of play—beginner to master players. You can find inexpensive books on chess or chess games in stores selling used books.

The *New York Times* has chess games every Sunday and Tuesday. Many local papers run chess columns every week. Check for them in your area. It's cool to play the games over on your own chessboard.

When beautiful chess happens:

We read it in the newspaper.
We see it in a book.
We see it on the Internet.
Big crowds come.
We smile.

Chess Terms

Here are some words used by chess players, and their meanings. Some common chess symbols are here, too. You will see these terms and symbols when you look at games in books, magazines, or newspapers.

Algebraic notation This system, or code, is used by chess players to write down their games. It's often called just "algebraic," for short. This system uses capital letters for the major pieces, lowercase letters for the rank and file squares, and symbols for the game moves.

Attack Threatening to win a piece or the game.

Castle A special double move to protect the King. This move can only be used when both the King and the Rook are still in their original positions on the board.

Check A King is in danger. Can he escape?

Checkmate Also simply "mate." The checked King is trapped.

Closed file Pawns are in the way. The pieces can't sweep across the board. Opposite of open file.

Defense Protecting our pieces, the squares, and the game. Openings are named "defenses" when Black made a special move in response to an attack by White.

Discovered Check If a piece is moved, the King is discovered to be in check behind it.

Double Check A check by two different pieces.

Draw Both players agree that no one can win. The game is ended.

Endgame Finishing off your opponent, getting checkmate.

En passant Also written just with initials, as e.p. This is when a pawn captures another pawn "in passing," as if the opponent's pawn had only moved one square instead of two on its first move.

Exchange You take an opponent's piece, and your opponent immediately takes your capturing piece. If the piece you took is worth more, you've "won the exchange."

File Each vertical (up and down) column on the chessboard, known by the letters "a" through "h."

Fork When a piece attacks two pieces at once.

Hanging A piece that has no defense and will be captured is said to be hanging.

Long diagonal The diagonal lines connecting two opposite corners of the board—X-shape. All the squares on each diagonal line are the same color, either black or white.

Open file No pawns are in the way. Pieces can move freely from one side of the board to the other. Opposite of closed file.

Opponent The person you are playing against.

Overworked When a piece is doing too much in a game. Other pieces are being ignored.

Pawn The pawn is not considered a "piece" and has no symbol. It is identified by its letter file and the square that it is on.

Piece The chess pieces are the Knight, the Rook, the Bishop, the Queen, and the King. The pawn is not counted as a piece, but it can become a Queen or any other piece if it reaches the other side of the board.

Pin A piece or pawn can't move—is pinned—because the King or some other piece would be placed in danger.

Postmortem Players reviewing moves after the game is over.

Rank Each horizontal (across) row on the chessboard, known by the numbers "1" through "8."

Refute This means saying "Ha, you thought that was a good move. Guess what, it isn't." You prove your opponent has made a mistake.

Resign Give up the game—seeing no way to win.

Sacrifice Sometimes simply called "sac," as in "to sac a piece." You give something up on purpose, to get something even better. If it is accidental, it is not a sacrifice.

Skewer If a threatened piece moves, a piece behind it is attacked.

Stalemate One player or the other has no legal move. The King cannot be "mated." No one wins.

Symbols Notation symbols for game moves: x = captures, + = check, ++ = checkmate (the end of the game), ! = good move, !! = great move, ? = bad move, ?? = rotten move, ?! = may be bad, !? = interesting move, 0-0 = castle kingside, 0-0-0 = castle queenside.

Trade An exchange of like pieces, usually pawns: take one, lose one.

About the Authors

Rosalyn B. Katz started playing tournament chess after her son David began to play. As a concerned parent, she wrote an education bill to place chess into the New Jersey elementary schools at the second grade level. She has also helped advance the playing of chess into other areas of education. She is the author of *Start Playing Chess* (1996) published by Sterling.

Both her sons, Steven and David, are grown now. Roz writes corporate documents for large companies when she is not busy playing chess. She lives in Rockaway, New Jersey, with Charles J. Pole…and their two cats, Cyd and Casey.

David L. Katz has been playing chess since he was three years old. He won his first trophy in a New York State scholastic tournament when he was six. He now works at Merrill Lynch Corporation in New York City.

David lives in West New York, New Jersey, with his wife Lynel.

Index